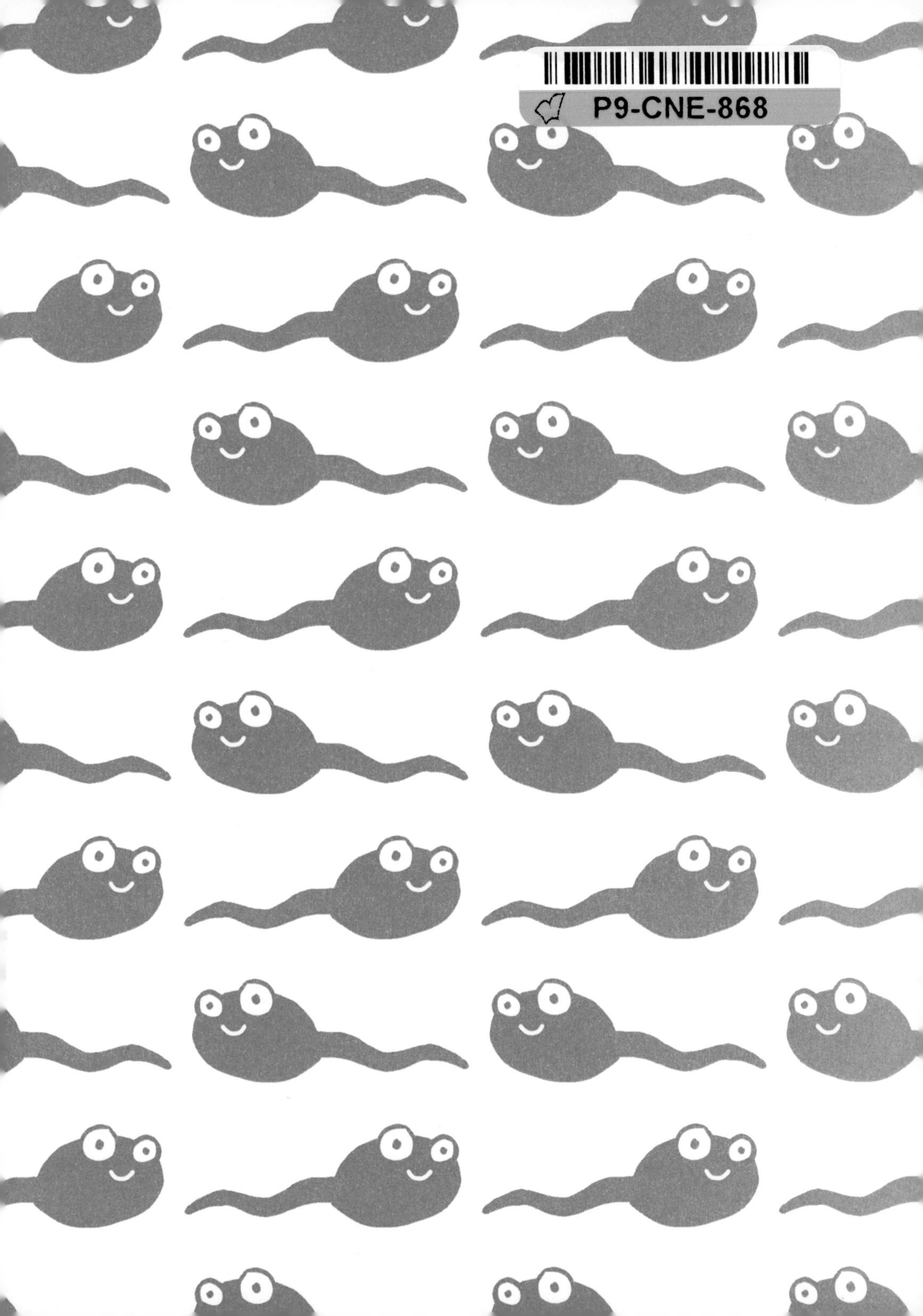

THE TOAD

For Frédérique and Léa-Rose

Published in Canada by Tundra Books, an imprint of Penguin Random House Canada Young Readers, a Penguin Random House Company

Library and Archives Canada Cataloguing in Publication

Gravel, Elise, author
        The toad / Elise Gravel.

(Disgusting critters)
Issued in print and electronic formats.
ISBN 978-1-77049-667-5 (bound).—ISBN 978-1-77049-669-9 (epub)

        I. Toads—Juvenile literature. I. Title. II. Series: Gravel, Elise
Disgusting critters.

QL668.E227G72 2016   j597.8'7   C2015-904008-6
                                             C2015-904009-4

Published simultaneously in the United States of America by Tundra Books of Northern New York, an imprint of Penguin Random House Canada Young Readers, a Penguin Random House Company

Library of Congress Control Number: 2015947649

Edited by Samantha Swenson
Designed by Elise Gravel and Tundra Books
The artwork in this book was rendered digitally.
Printed and bound in China

www.penguinrandomhouse.ca

4 5 6   22 21 20 19

Penguin
Random House
TUNDRA BOOKS

Elise Gravel

THE TOAD

GREETINGS !

tundra

Ladies and gentlemen, give a warm
round of applause for our friend

THE TOAD.

Hi, HOW
ARE YOU ?

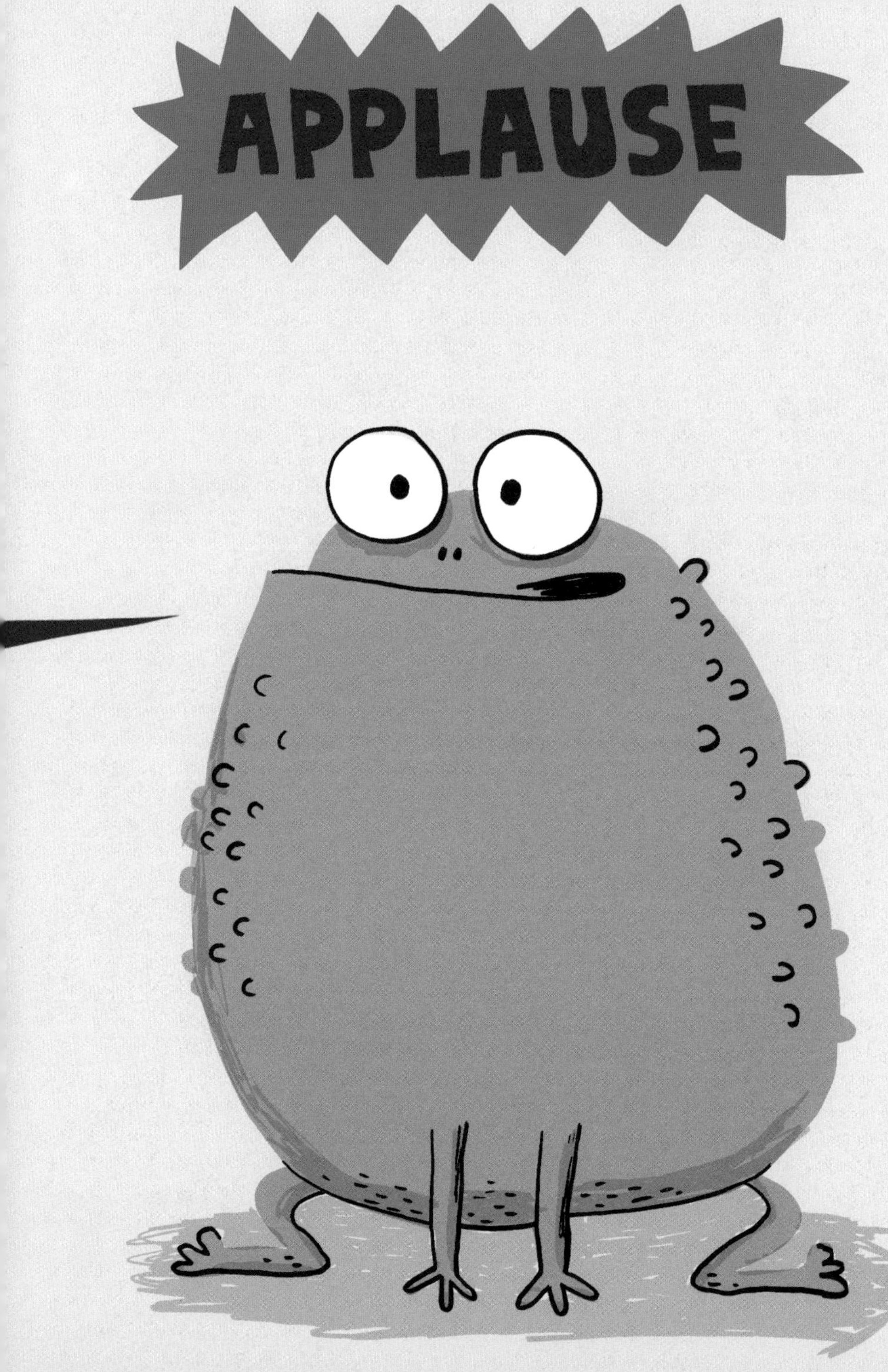
APPLAUSE

The toad is a type of

FROG,

but with some special traits.

Toads and frogs are both descended from a frog who lived millions of years ago in South America.

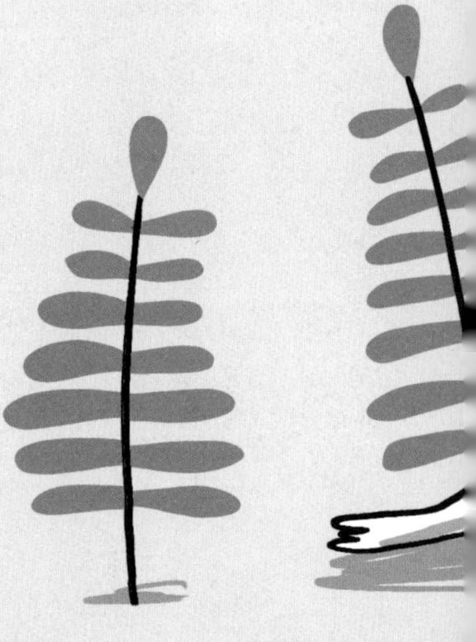

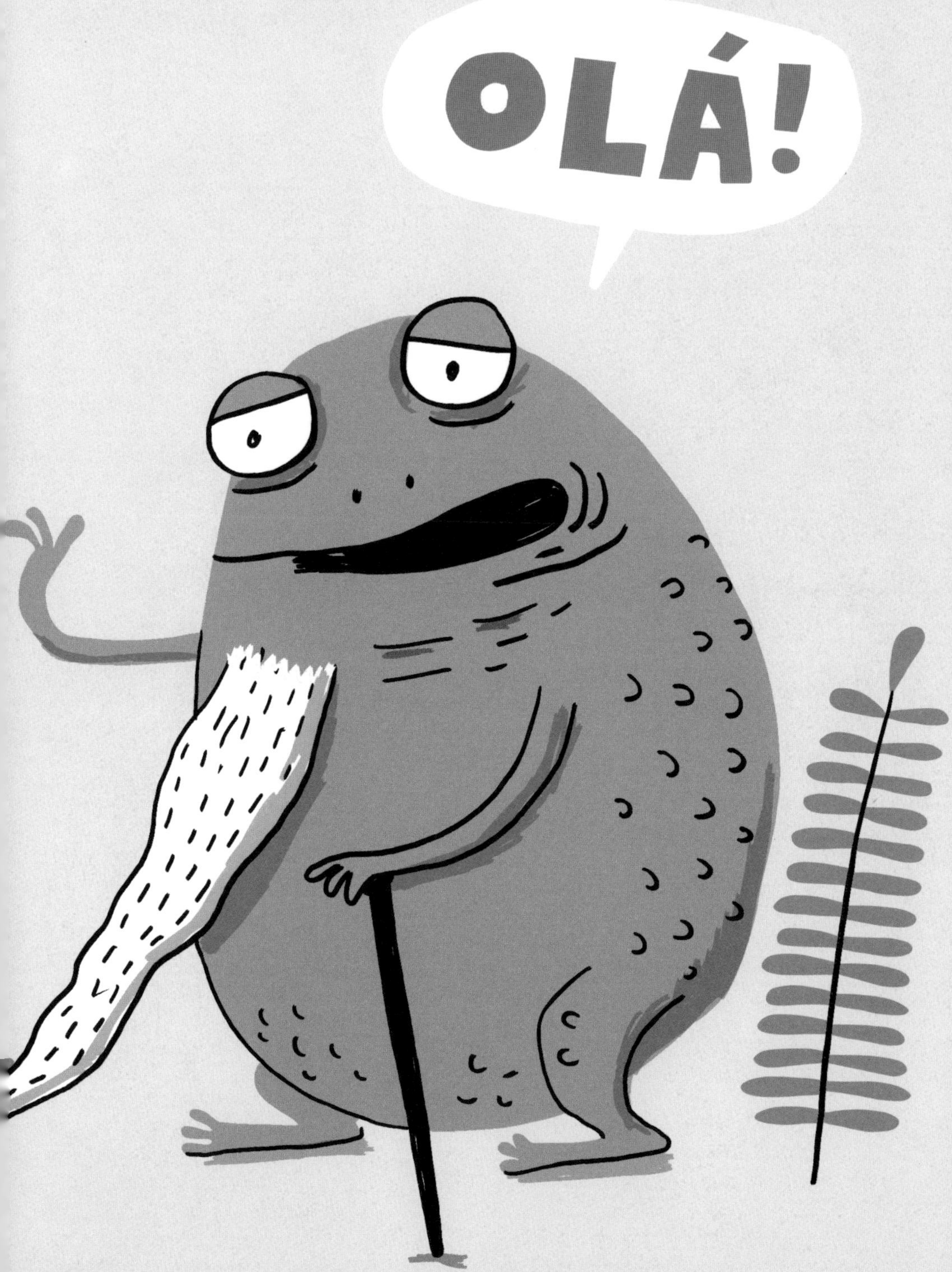
OLÁ!

There are more than

5,000

species of toads and frogs.

Some live in water,

some in trees

and some on the ground.

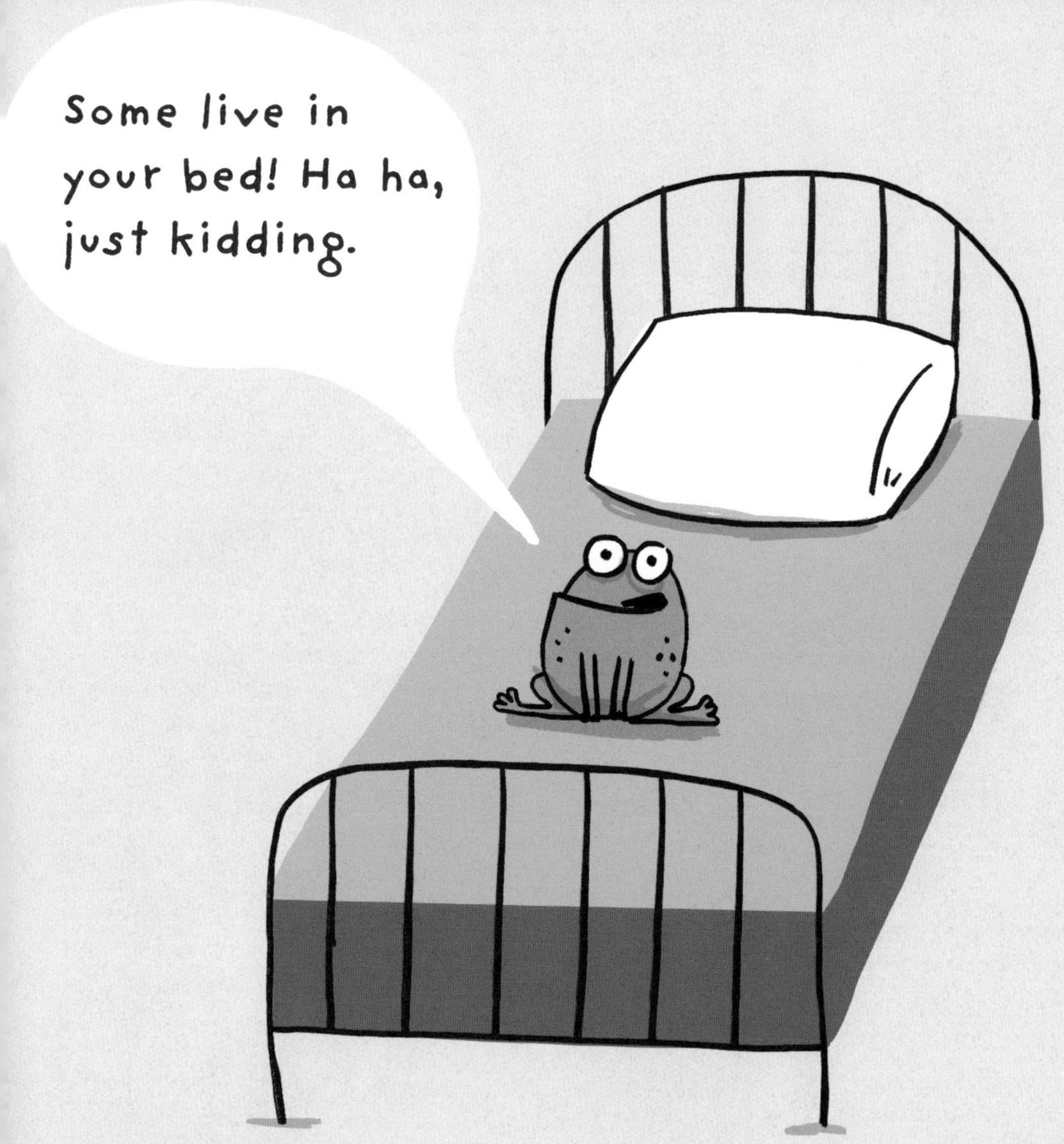
Some live in your bed! Ha ha, just kidding.

Toads are frogs that live on land and have drier skin, shorter legs and stouter bodies.

Some toads are really

WEiRD!

The Emei mustache toad:
It grows a mustache
made of spikes.

Hey ladies!

I'm not
here.

The Venezuela pebble toad:
It disguises itself as a
pebble when threatened.

The Suriname toad: Her babies come out of her back!

Who's the boss?

The cane toad: It can grow as big as 15 inches (38 centimeters).

Hi there!

In this book, we'll be talking about Bufo bufo, or the common toad.

The toad's skin is very special:
she drinks and breathes through it!
She needs to keep her skin hydrated,
so she lives where she has access to

WATER.

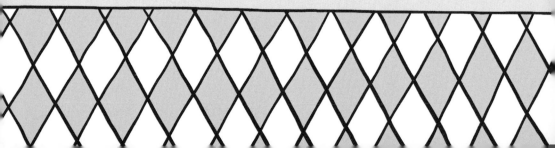

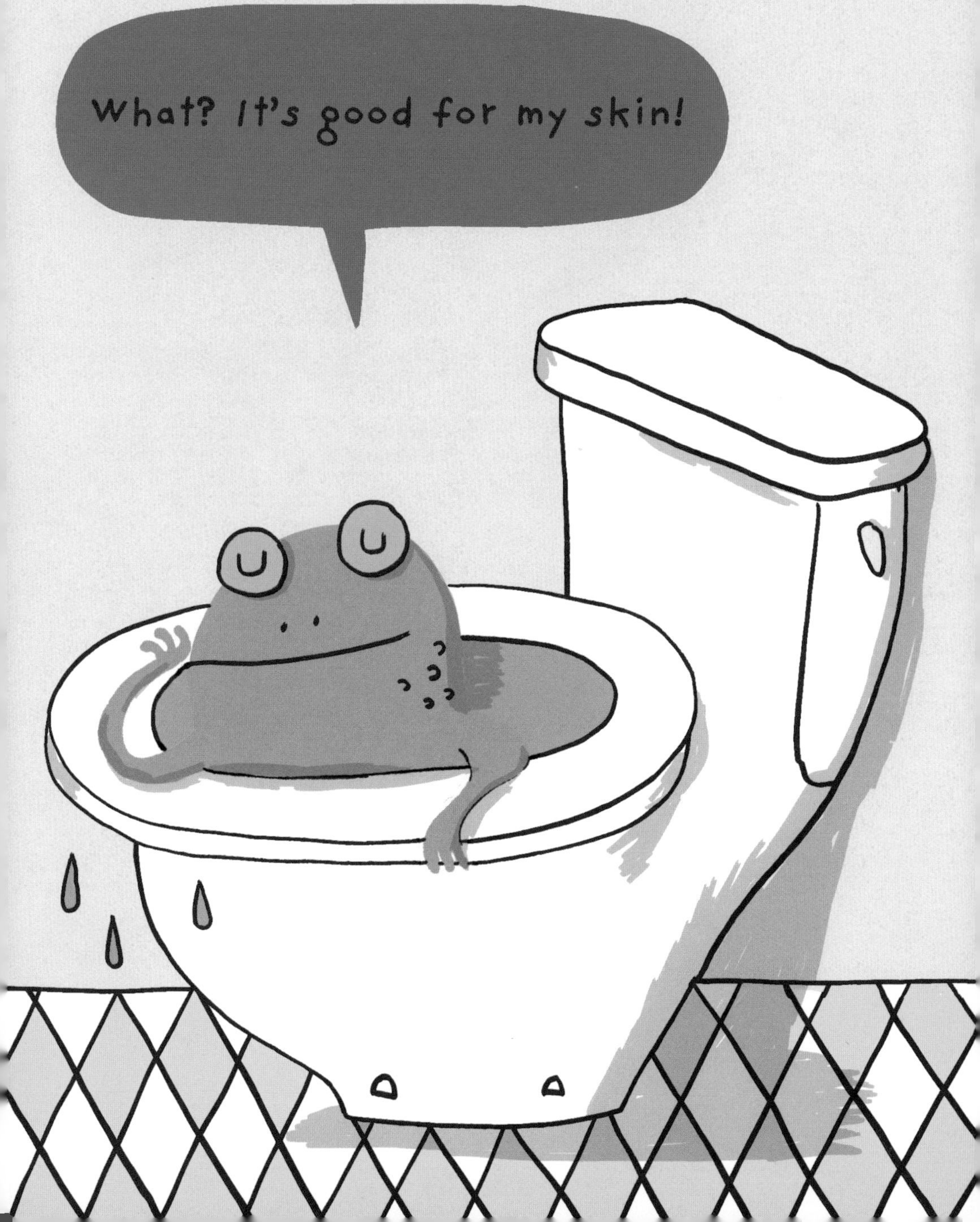
What? It's good for my skin!

The toad eats mostly bugs, worms and spiders. The toad is a pretty lazy hunter: she sits and waits for her

PREY

to walk by her, and then she catches it with her long tongue.

Tralalala.

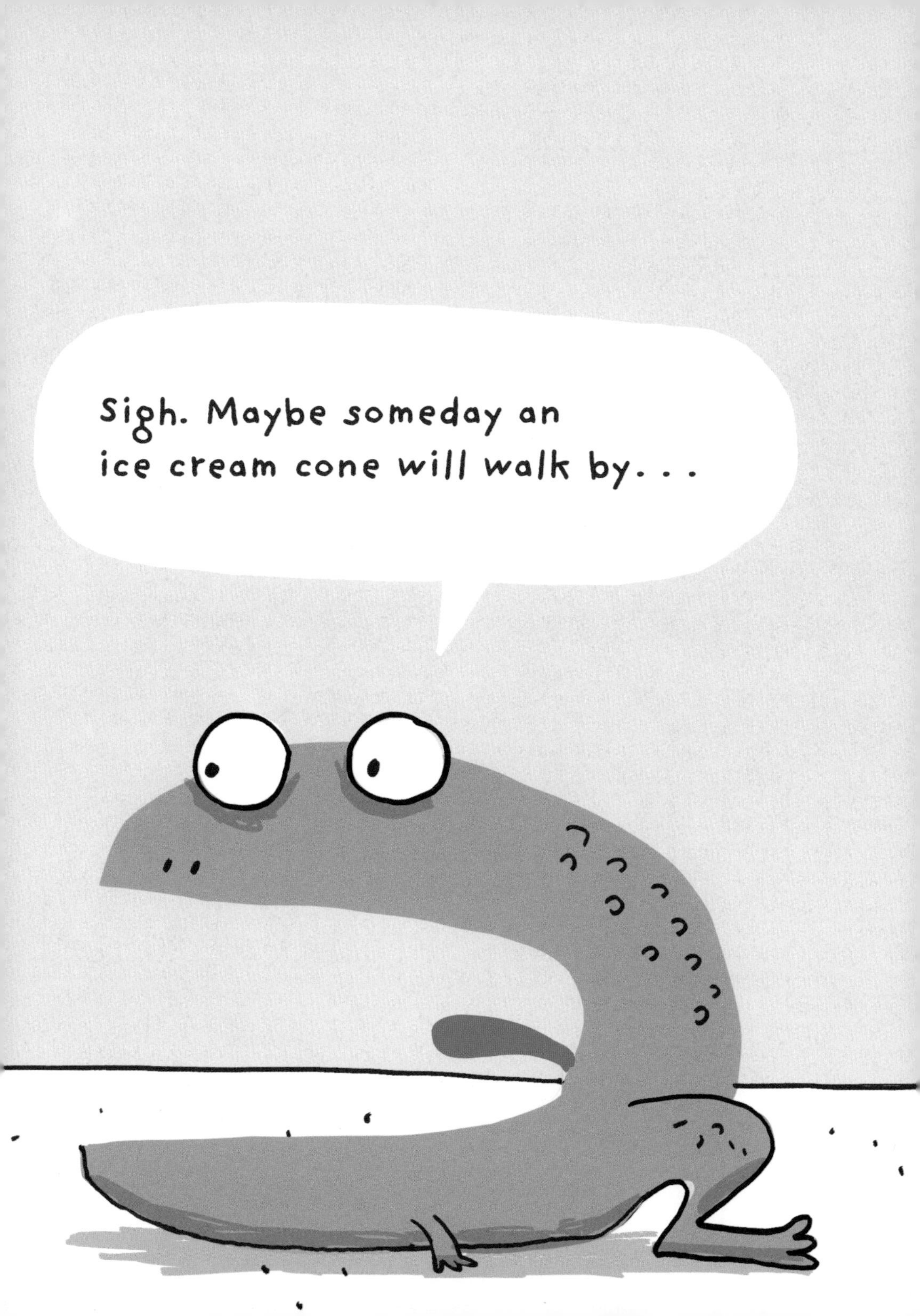
Sigh. Maybe someday an ice cream cone will walk by. . .

The toad sometimes sheds her skin to keep it healthy, and that's kind of gross. It means she gets rid of the old skin, and then . . . SHE EATS IT!

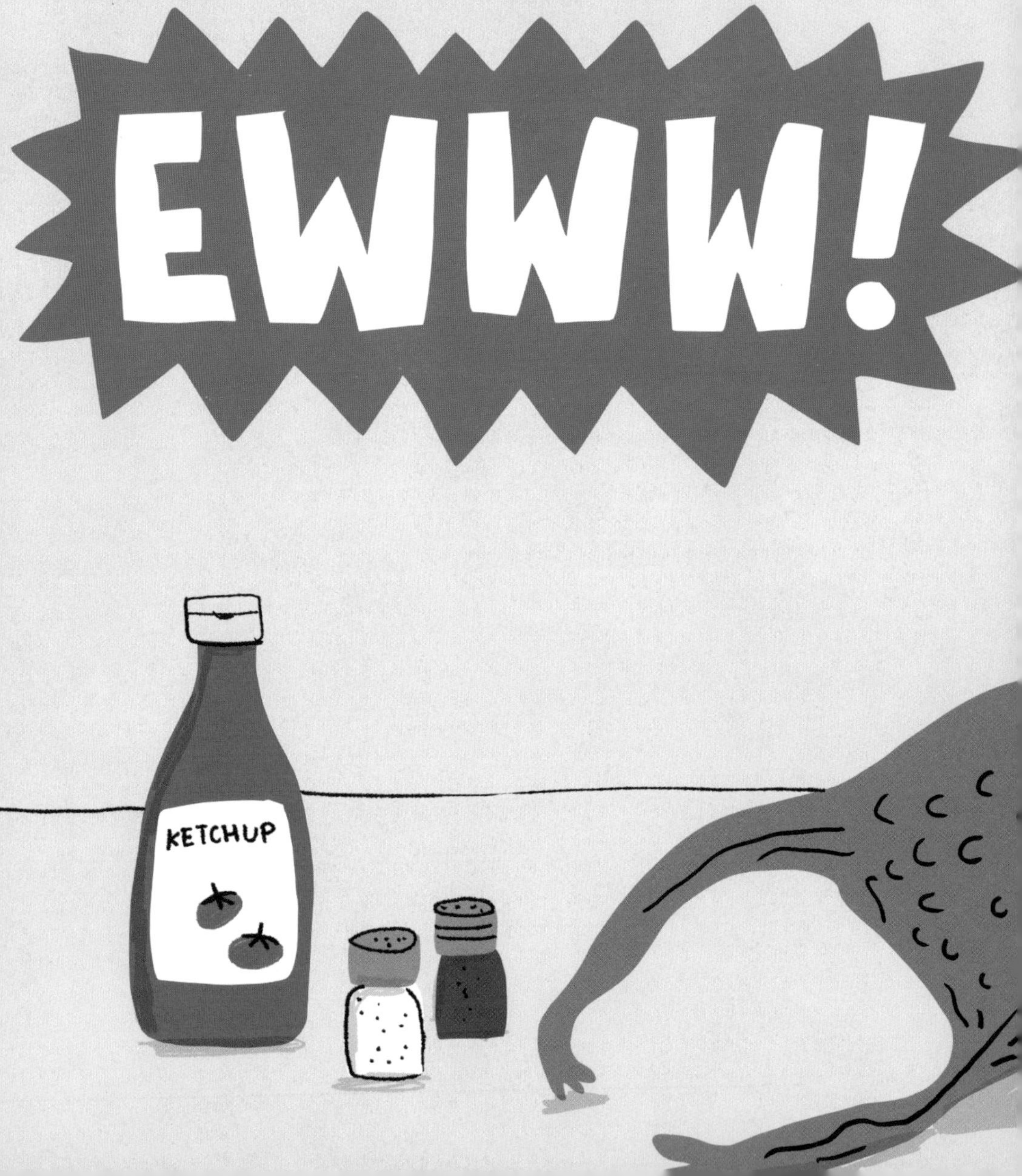
EWWW!
KETCHUP

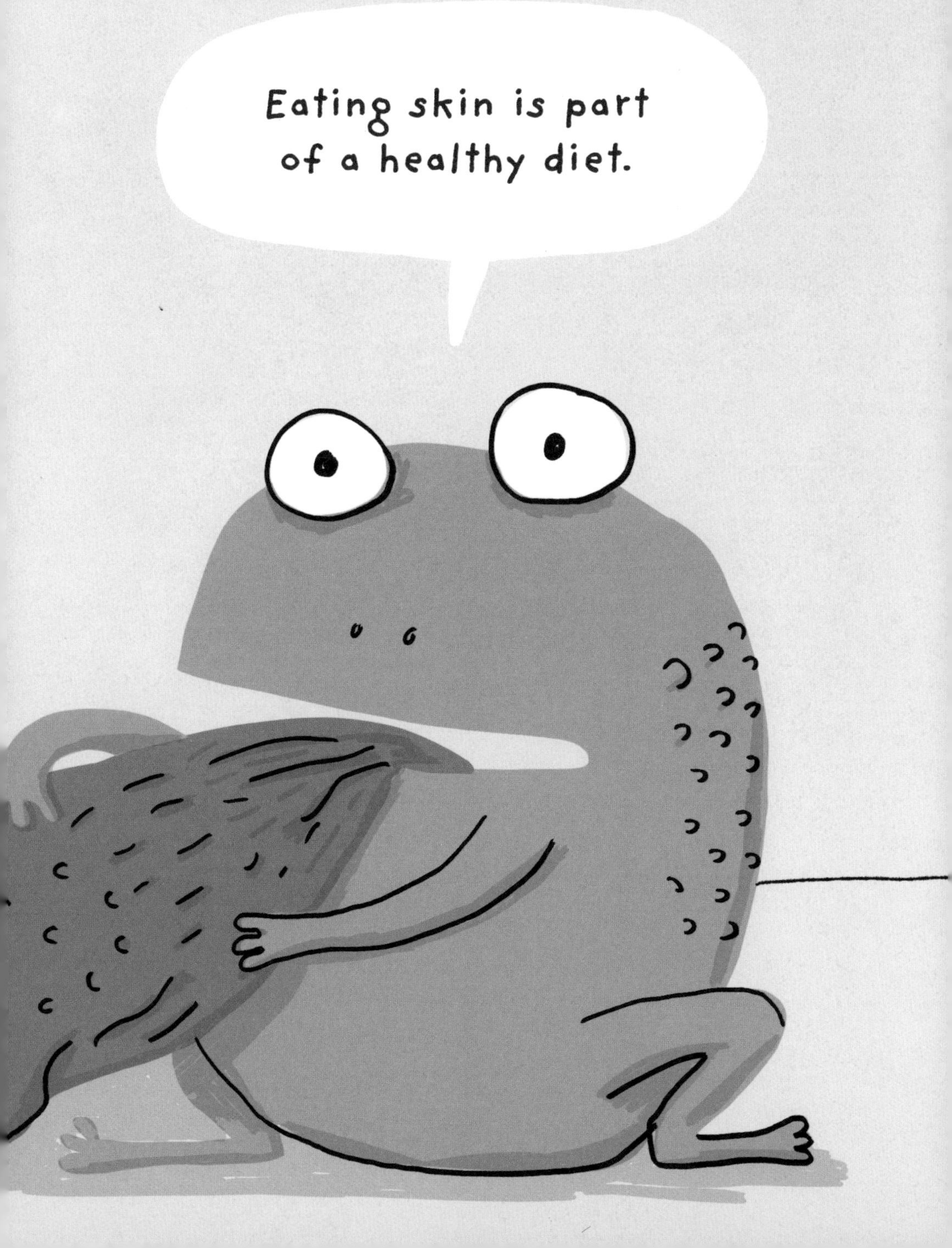
Eating skin is part of a healthy diet.

When the toad is threatened, she releases a

through her skin to ward off
predators—it tastes disgusting!
Some toad species put out a toxin so
strong it can be deadly.

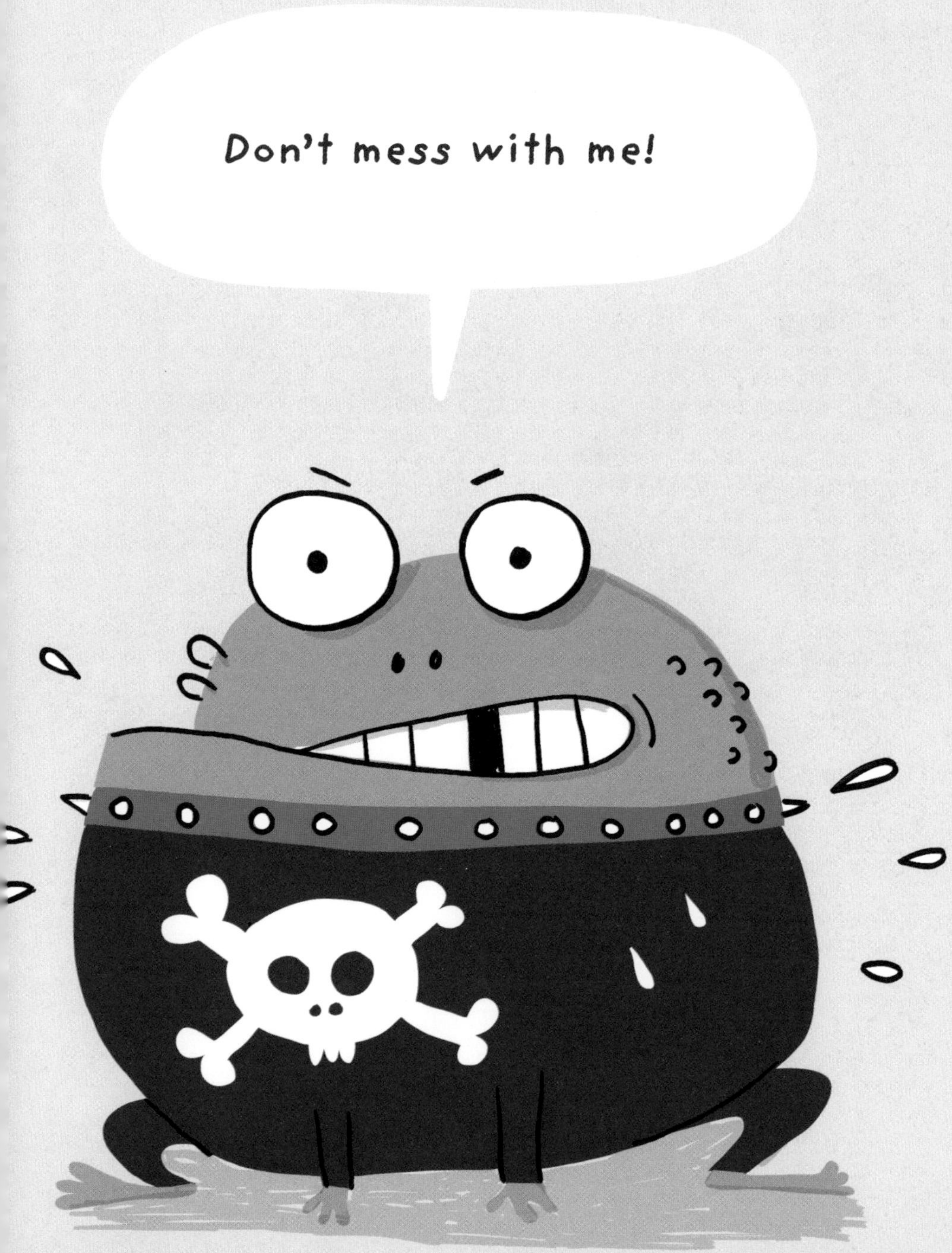
Don't mess with me!

We often call the bumps on the toad's back "warts," but they're not actually warts. They are just bumps on her skin that help her

with the ground.

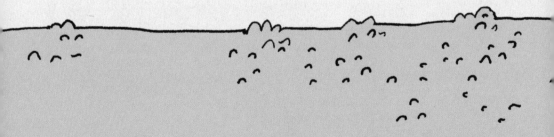

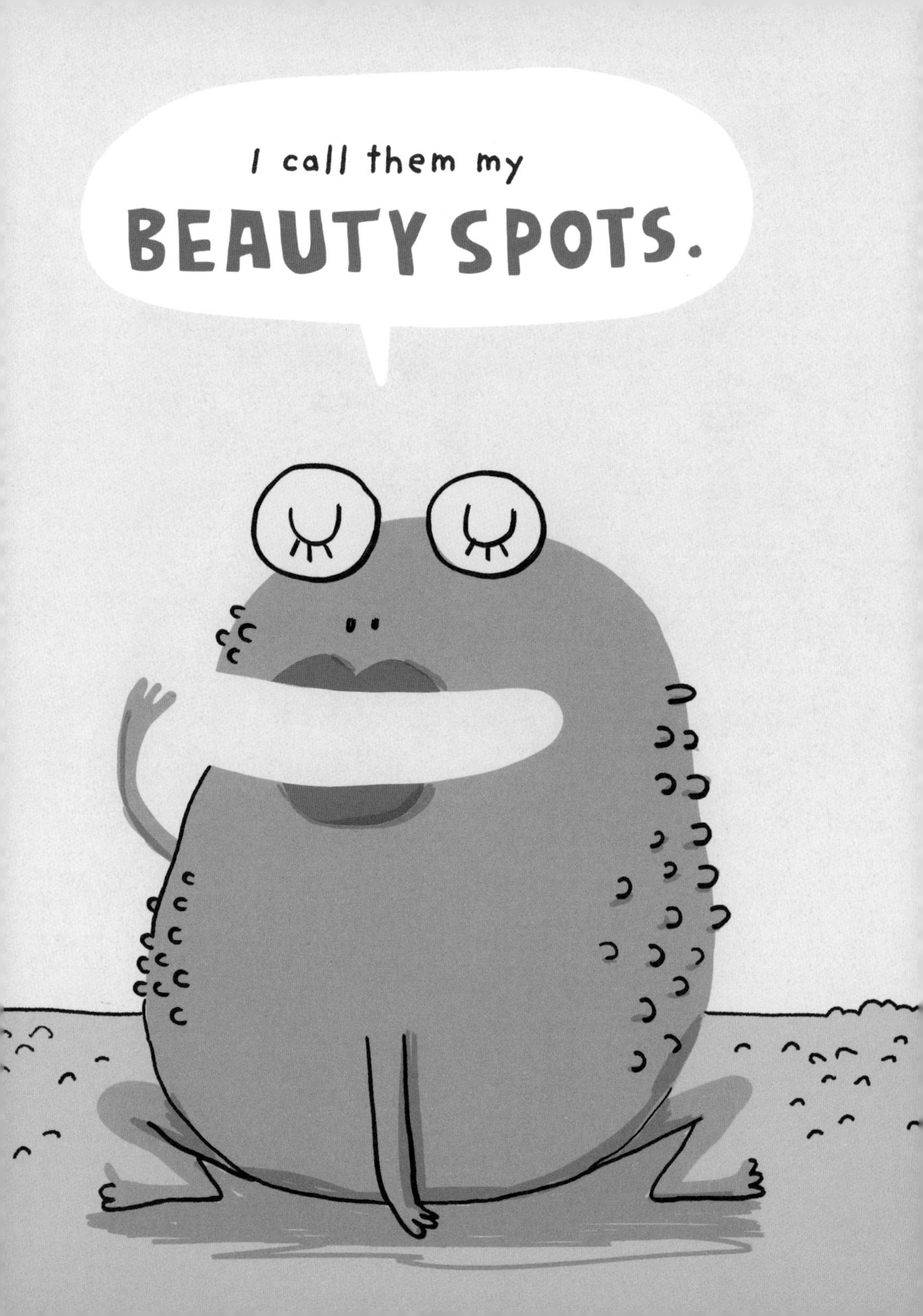
I call them my
BEAUTY SPOTS.

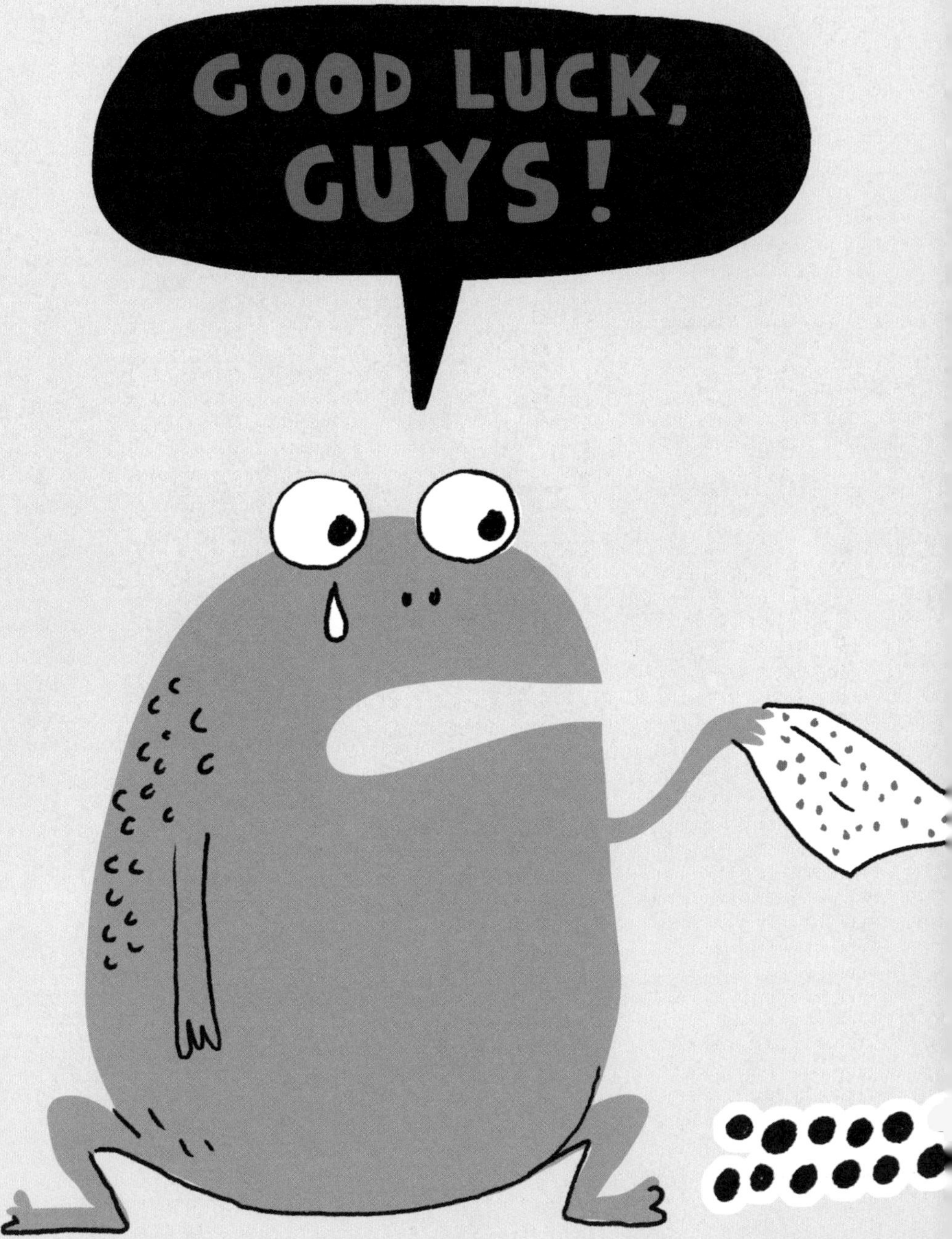
GOOD LUCK, GUYS!

The toad lays her eggs in the water, as many as

at a time. She lays them in very long strings in shallow water. The eggs face many dangers, including being eaten by hungry animals. Only a few lucky toads will make it.

Baby toads are called

TADPOLES.

They're pretty cute, huh?

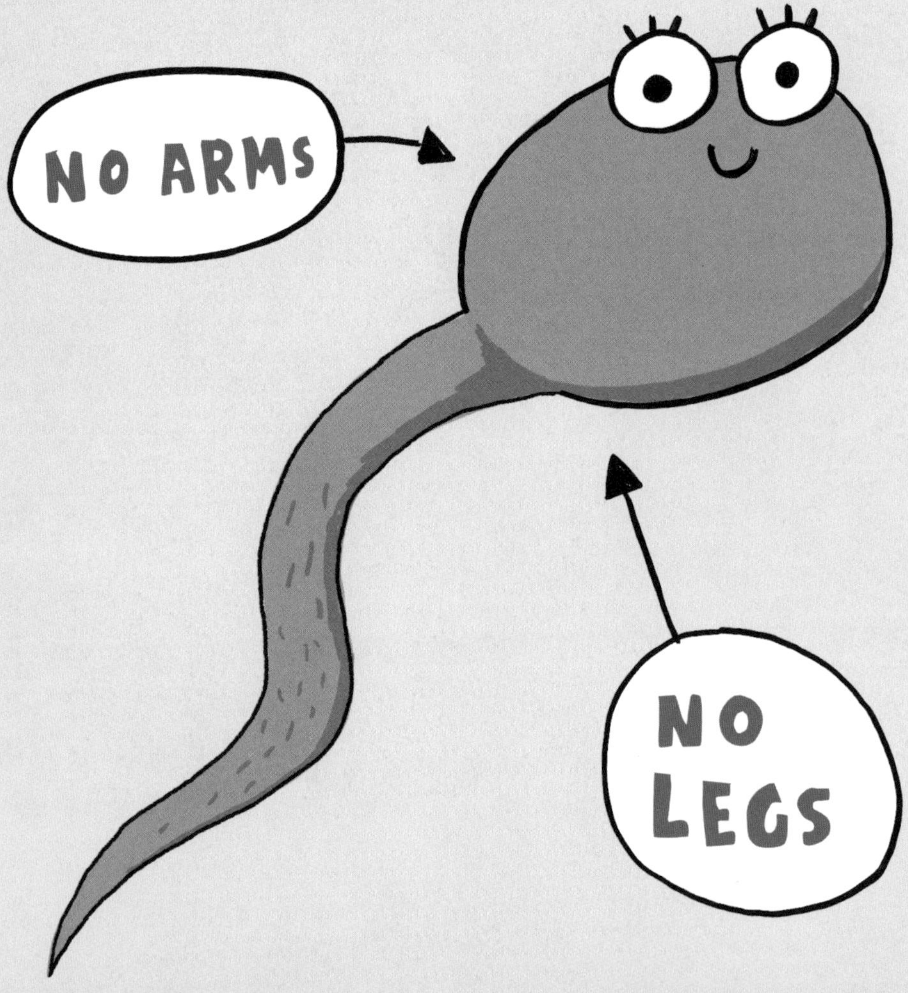
NO ARMS
NO LEGS

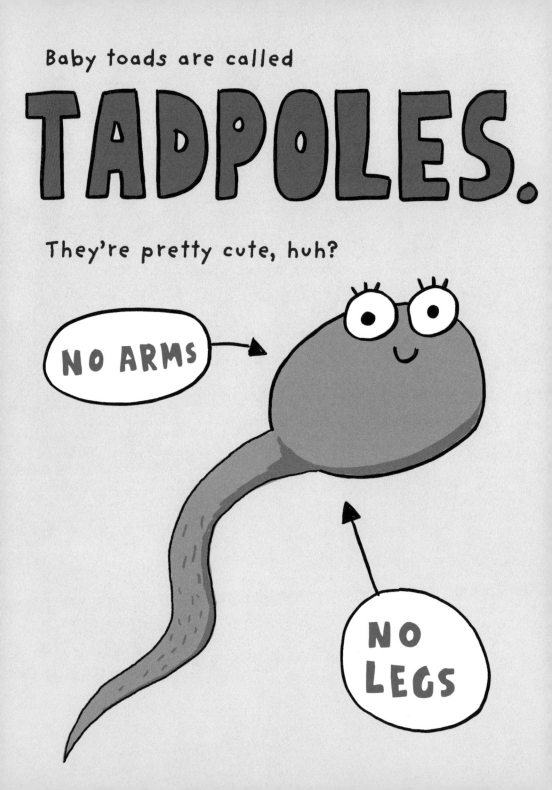

The tadpoles are born and live underwater for 8 to 12 weeks, until their legs have grown and their tails have disappeared. Then they move onto land, where they can live up to 12 years.

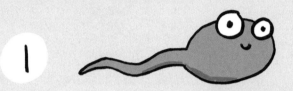

1

2

3

4

The toad is very useful to humans because she eats lots of pests that can be harmful to crops.

Healthy toads are a sign of a

environment, since they can only live in a clean, natural habitat.

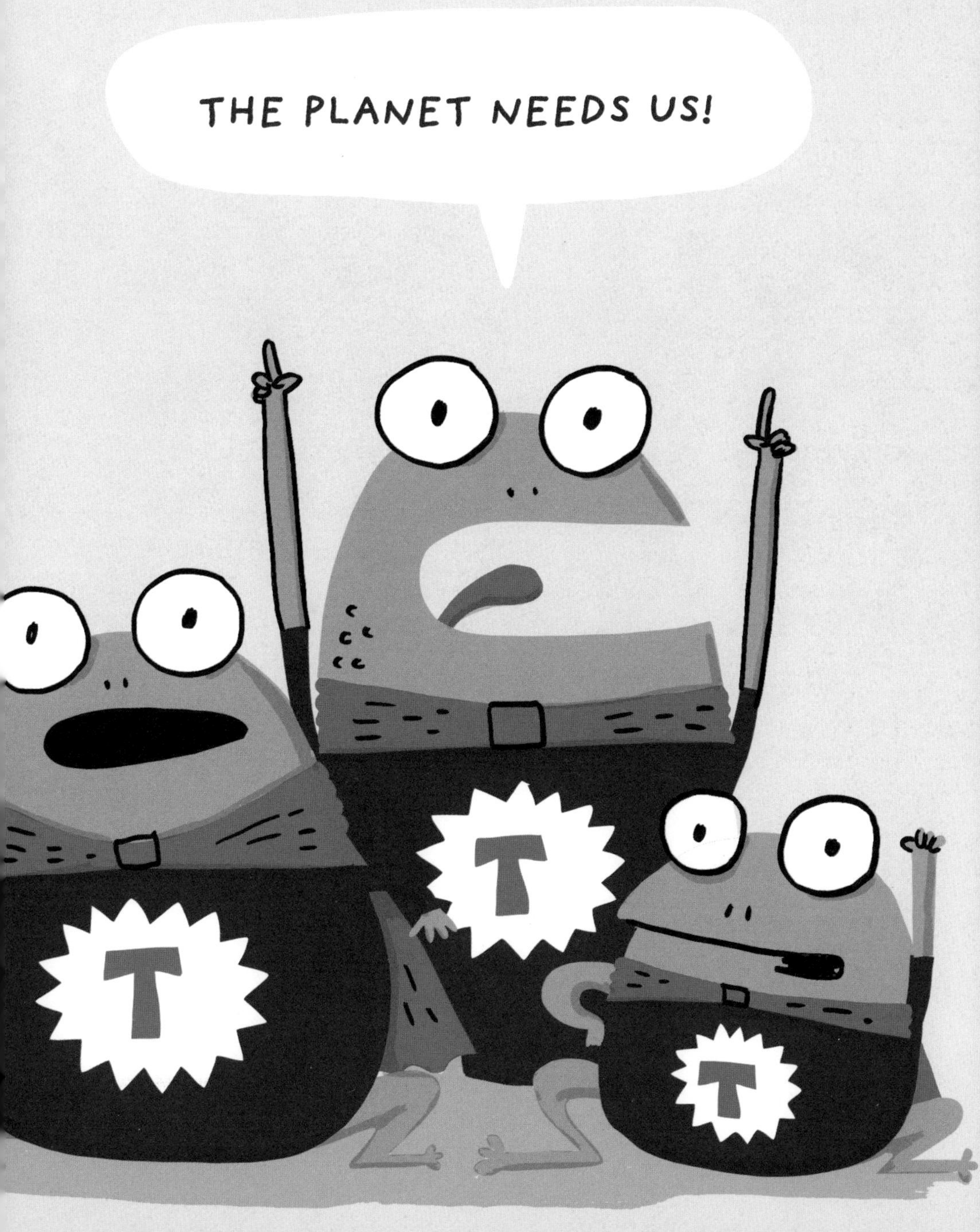
THE PLANET NEEDS US!

Unfortunately, there are fewer and fewer toads around the earth. Some species are endangered and some are extinct. This could be because of

POLLUTiON,

the use of pesticides, global warming or the destruction of their habitats by humans.

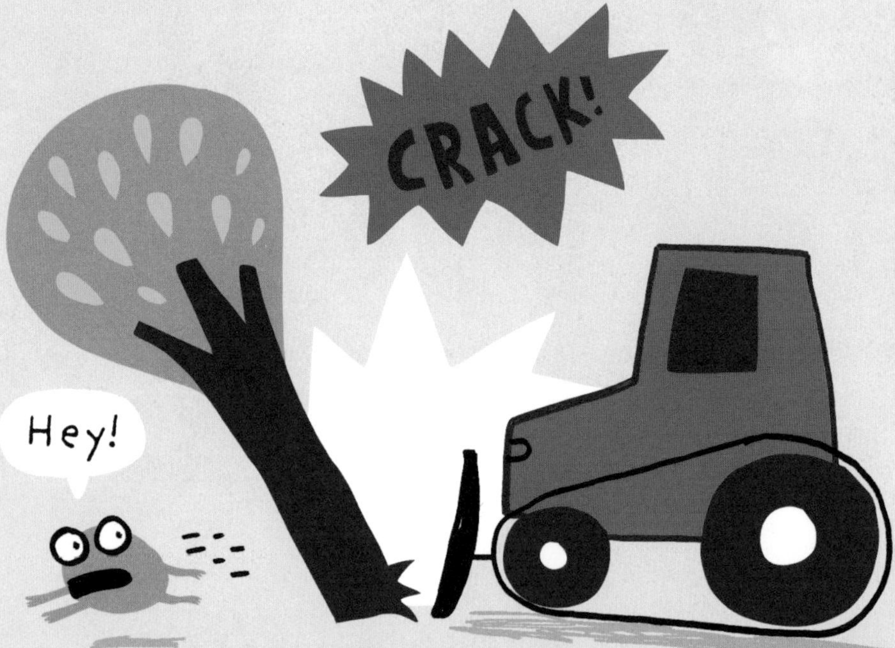
CRACK!
Hey!

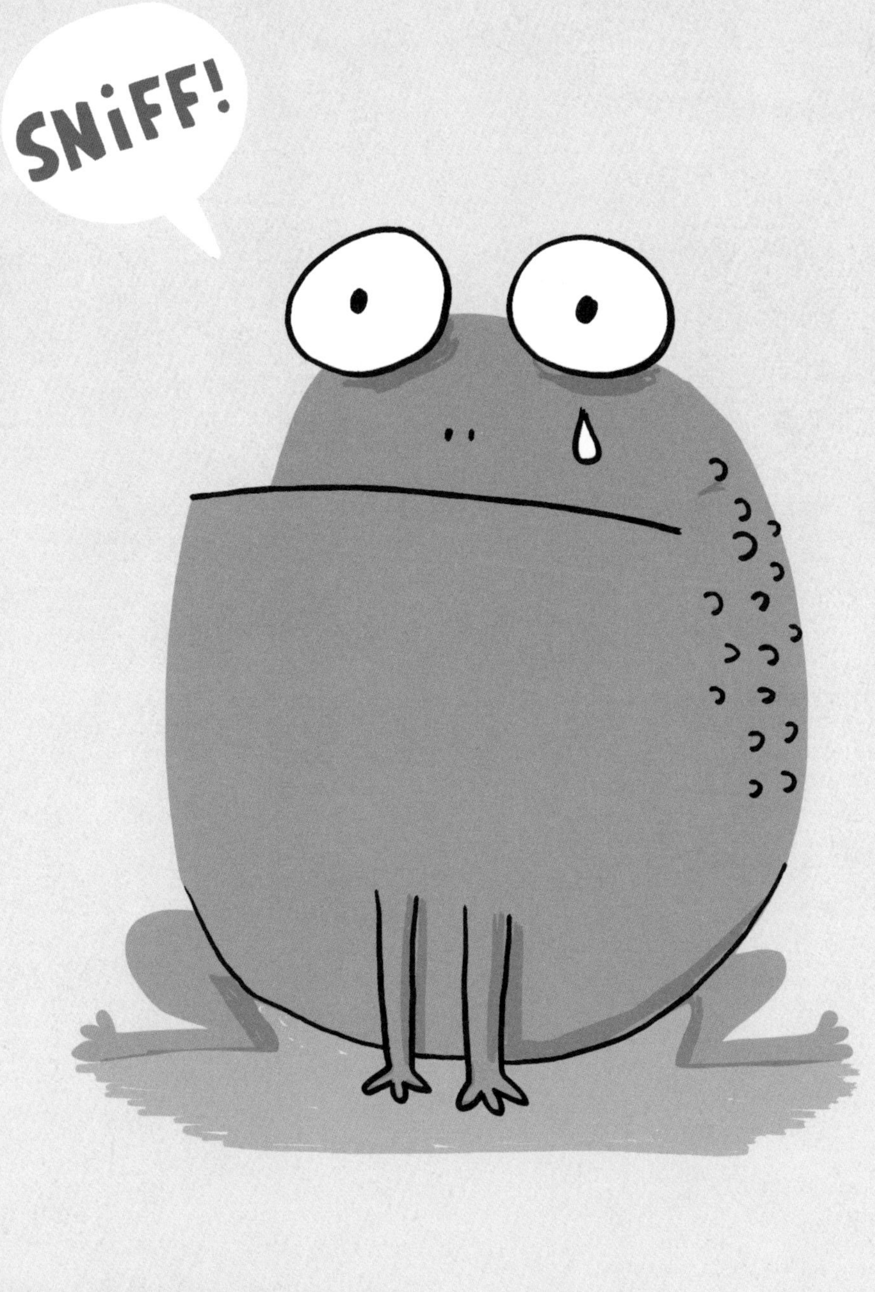
SNiFF!

*This information is sad, so I won't make a joke here.

So remember to keep our planet clean!
The toad is our friend and she
needs your

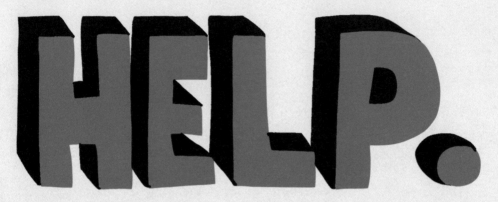

HELP.

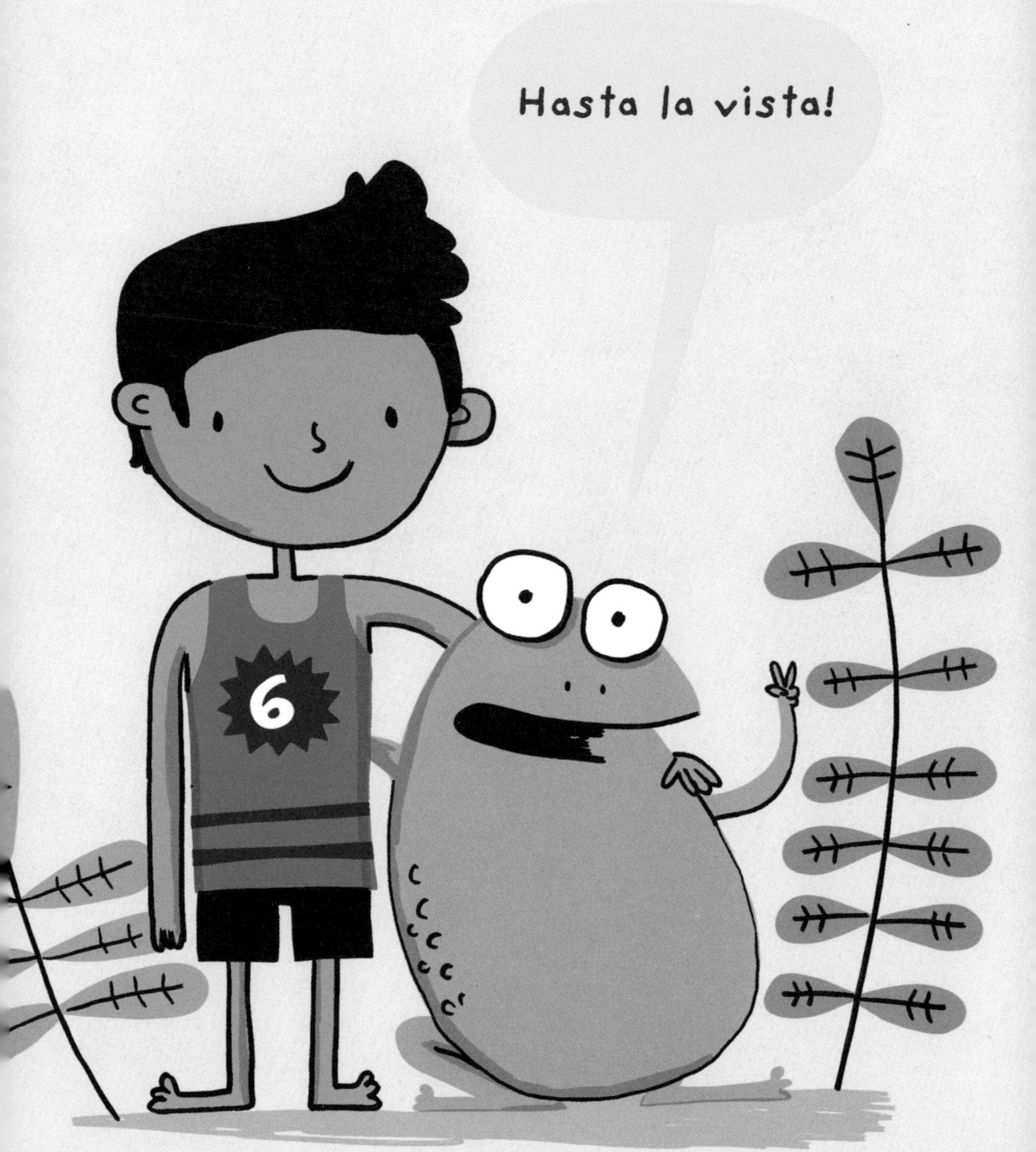
Hasta la vista!

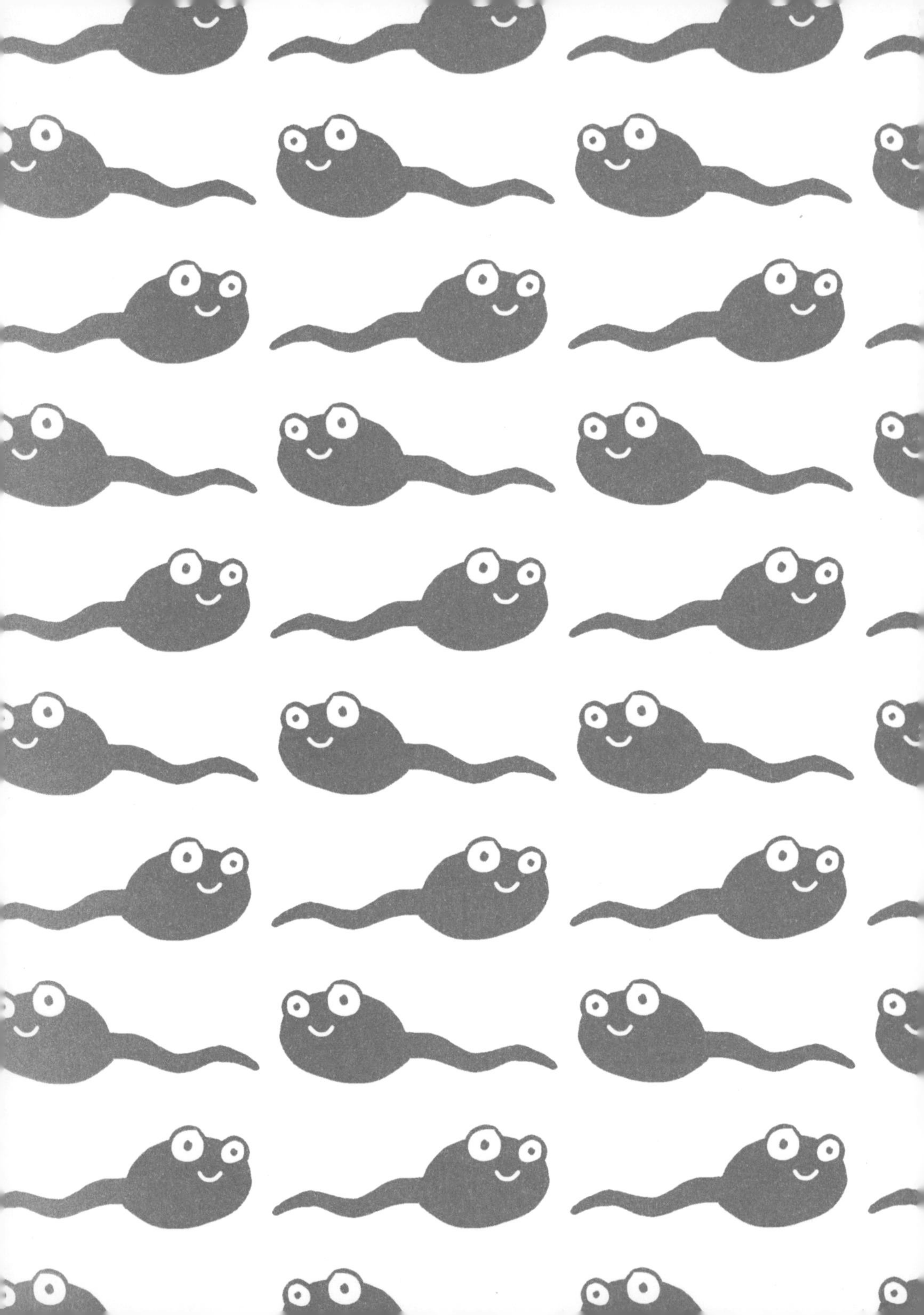